WOMEN LIVING HOLY FOR GOD

"A BIBLE STUDY & DISCUSSION GUIDE FOR WOMEN"

DR. TIMMY L. SYKES

WOMEN LIVING HOLY FOR GOD

SYKES PUBLISHING,
CHATTANOOGA, TN

WOMEN LIVING HOLY FOR GOD

HOLY
WOMEN

Dr. Timmy Lundale Sykes

Copyright © 2005 by Timmy L. Sykes

Introduction

As I read through the book of Luke over and over in preparation for this study, I was struck with the shepherd's heart that Jesus has for us. I realized that in many ways I felt like a wandering sheep that just needed Jesus to carry me home.

If you are like me, stressed with the busyness of life and even distracted by ministry demands, drink in the life of the Savior through your daily study time. Put it at the top of your list of priorities. Ask God to speak to you through each day's lesson, through your small group discussion, and through the weekly lectures and studies.

As you read the age-old story of Jesus, let it come alive to you. Consider what it must have been like to walk and talk with Him on the dusty roads of Galilee. Imagine yourself among the crowds of people pushing to get up close to the itinerant Teacher. See yourself grieving at the cross and exultant upon recognizing the Risen Lord.

In this study guide, I tell life stories of different women that I had the opportunity to interview while writing this Bible Study and Discussion Guide...

May the Lord richly bless your study! May it truly be a time of coming home!

Pastor Tim Sykes
November, 2004

Dedication

This Bible Study and Discussion Guide is dedicated to Mrs. L. Quinetta Norma, a Beloved Woman of God, and Inspirational, Motivational Missionary infused with the God blessed gift of teaching, singing and speaking! I appreciate your thoughtfulness to utilize this Study Guide to teach women about the HOLINESS of God!

I really appreciate your boldness and passion you display, and your dedication to serve God and His people daily!

May the love of God, the joy of Jesus, and the sweet communion of the Holy Spirit rest, rule and abide with you always!

Love,

Dr. Timmy L. Sykes

How to Use this Study Guide

This study is designed to help you consistently spend time in God's Word. You will gain the most from this study if you do it day by day, answering just that day's questions, rather than trying to stuff it all in at once. Each week's lesson is divided into five days of homework to encourage you to listen daily to His voice. The Bible is God's message to you, and He wants to speak with you personally.

Unless instructed otherwise, use only the Scriptures to answer the questions. Rather than go to commentaries or even the notes in a study Bible, ask God to give you insight from His Word.

A Precious Word from God —Each week you will have a verse to memorize that brings out an essential lesson or thought from the week's study. Begin learning it the first day. You might copy it on an index card and carry it with you throughout the week, hiding God's Word in your heart.

Sharing questions are designed for you to write stories, insights, and applications from your own life. If we are to be in community with one another and support one another, we must truly know one another. You will never be forced to share one of these answers aloud with your group.

Responding to God questions are reminders that we study God's Word so that He can speak to us and we are changed thereby. We should be listening for His voice. These types of questions ask for a response to God's personal message to you. I have found that writing out my prayers helps me to focus better on what I need to say to God. No one will ask you to read yours, but you should always feel free to share your response with your group.

Diamonds in the Word are optional questions designed for those who want to dig deeper. Some of the answers will be easy for even a beginning Bible student to answer, and some will require more experience in God's Word. As a group you will not discuss these, but the background that you gain from digging into God's Word in a deeper way will certainly enrich your personal study.

PERSONAL STORIES

Each lesson includes a true story that relates the truths of that week's lesson to a woman's real life   experience. Some of the names have been changed to protect the guilty! These stories will encourage you in your walk with God and your growth in godliness.

Dr. Tim Sykes

Coming Home to Jesus

Week One—Prepare your Heart to Come Home

A PRECIOUS WORD FROM GOD

"He who is mighty has done great things for me, and holy is His name."

Mary in Luke 1:49 (NET)

INTRODUCTION

Do you long to come home—the place of love, companionship, rest, peace, and security? Perhaps this is the kind of home you can only long for, never having been able to enjoy such a place here on earth. Picture a home where Jesus waits for you. Will you choose to spend time there with Him? Although salvation is a free gift that we can never lose, believers do not always enjoy the blessings of being at home with Jesus on this earth. As you read His story, drink in His presence and enjoy His beauty, the beauty of God Himself. It is possible to come home while we wait to go "home"!

This week we look at Jesus' early life and preparation for ministry. Although our lesson is long, covering more than three chapters of the book of Luke, the stories will be familiar to you. Attempt to read them as if you were reading them for the first time. Put yourself in the places of the characters. See the sights and smell the scents of first century Israel. Focus on God, and come home to all that He is!

DAY ONE STUDY

Read Luke 1:1-4.

1. Luke outlines his reason, or purpose for writing this book here in the preface. What is it?

2. The NIV and the NET translations of the Bible use the word "fulfilled" in v. 1 where the NASB uses the word "accomplished". What does the word fulfilled suggest about the events that Luke relates in his book?

Read Luke 1:5-25.

3. What prophecies are given to Zechariah about his son (vv. 13-17)?

4. How would you have felt if you were Zechariah? Why?

Read Luke 1:26-56.

5. What qualities do you see in Mary as you read through this passage? What does the text say that leads you to these insights about her?

Mary's words in Luke 1:46-56, often interpreted as poetic or hymnic, are traditionally called the Magnificat, from the Latin for "My soul magnifies the Lord," the first line of the song. Our memory verse this week is from Mary's psalm. Begin to memorize it now.

- **Diamonds in the Word:** Mary's psalm is filled with similarities to Hannah's song in 1 Samuel 2:1-10. What parallels do you observe as you compare these passages? What does this reveal about Mary?

6. **Sharing question:** Sometimes God asks us to take on difficult assignments, just as He did Mary. Life situations such as broken families, difficult employers, or failing health challenge our faith. There are times when God brings trials, which are not caused by our own mistakes or sins, into our lives. God does this for a reason, just as He asked Mary to be pregnant outside of marriage in order to bless the whole world. Share with your group a difficult situation from the past or one which you are experiencing right now that you did not bring about through your own doing. What do you learn from Mary's example that could have helped you?

7. **Responding to God:** Write a prayer of praise based upon Mary's psalm. In it, deal with a specific situation that you are facing today. Drink in the beauty of the Lord's character, and see yourself at home with Him.

DAY TWO STUDY

Read Luke 1:57-80.

Zechariah's praise psalm is called the "Benedictus", from the Latin of the first line.

- ***Diamonds in the Word:*** What Old Testament prophecies does Zechariah mention? Use your concordance to find the cross references and indicate where they are found in the Scriptures. It may be helpful to write these beside the Luke passage right in your Bible so that you can easily find them as you share Christ with others.

8. Focus on 1:78-79. Describe Zechariah's beliefs about what God would do for His people through the Messiah.

Read Luke 2:1-20, the often told story of Jesus' birth.

9. Trace the various emotions of the shepherds from vv. 8-20. They were the first people to announce the Messiah's birth.[1]

    Read Luke 2:21-40.

10. What insights do these verses give you about Joseph and Mary?

---

[1] Messiah is the Hebrew word for the Greek word Christ. Both mean "anointed one."

1. **Sharing Question:** What one quality do you see in either Simeon or Anna that you need in your life? What can you do to strengthen that area?

2. What truths about Jesus did God reveal to Simeon and Anna?

Read Luke 2:41-52.

3. How would you have felt in Joseph and Mary's situation both before and after they found Jesus?

4. **Sharing question:** Share one situation from the past or present with your group in which you experienced anxiety or unbelief because you didn't understand God's plan.

5. **Responding to God:** Write a prayer asking God to help you focus on His hope and His promises when your emotions and circumstances tempt you to unbelief. If you are dealing with such a situation currently, mention it specifically. God is waiting for you to come home to Him in faith.

Day Three Study

Read Luke 3:1-20.

6. Describe John the Baptist's preaching.

7. Write a definition of true repentance as you understand it from John's message.

8. Read John 1:19-28. From Luke and John's accounts of John the Baptist, what do you learn about his character?

9. How does the emphasis in John the Baptist's message prepare the way of the Lord, fulfilling the prophecy quoted from Isaiah 40:3-5?

10. *Sharing question:* What one area of your life is not prepared for Jesus' entrance so that you can truly be at home with Him? You may be refusing Him access so that you can run things as you please or simply because you think you can handle it. Perhaps you are harboring un-forgiveness or bitterness against someone who mistreated you. It may be that you are gossiping about a friend or employer behind her back. Perhaps you are fearful about the future because you want it to be your way rather than trusting God for His way. Whatever it is, share your struggle. You may want to write the struggle down as your prayer request to share with your small group.

11. *Responding to God:* Write a prayer based upon the struggle that you mentioned in the last question. Confess anything that is sin and open your heart and yield this area to the coming of Jesus' rule in your life so that you may truly know what it means to come home.

Read Luke 3:23-38, Jesus' genealogy.

• *Diamonds in the Word:* Compare this genealogy with the one in Mt. 1:1-17. Read in your commentaries and/or notes in your study Bible about the differences between the two. Explain your understanding.

DAY FOUR STUDY

Read Luke 4:1-13.

12. Why did Jesus go into the wilderness to be tempted?

13. How did Jesus' temptation, at this and other times in His life, prepare Him for ministry according to Hebrews 2:17-18; 4:14-15?

14. ***Sharing question:*** Share about a time of testing or temptation that God clearly brought into your life. Nothing you did put you in the situation. It may involve the temptation not to trust God or to reject Him.

Jesus was vulnerable to the first temptation because He had been fasting. The NET Bible comments:[2]

> The reference to Jesus eating nothing could well be an idiom meaning that he ate only what the desert provided; see Exod 34:28. A desert fast simply meant eating only what one could obtain in the desert. The parallel in Matt 4:2 speaks only of Jesus fasting.
>
> *NET Bible*

---

[2] *NET Bible: New English Translation*, Second Beta Edition, (Biblical Studies Press L.L.C.), Note 15, p. 1803.

I find that fatigue can be a huge factor when I sin with anger, impatience, or speaking when I should have kept my mouth shut. Also, I am more prone to sin in my own areas of weakness, just as you are. Such things as materialism, pride, or the desire for love can open us up to temptation.

15. *Sharing question:* In what situations are you more vulnerable to temptation? How can being aware of these areas of vulnerability help you overcome temptation? What can you do to protect yourself from areas where you are more vulnerable to sin?

16. In your own words, describe the three temptations of Jesus recorded in the Scriptures.

• *Diamonds in the Word:* How were these three temptations designed specifically for Jesus? How do they compare with the lusts of 1 John 2:16?

17. *Responding to God:* Pray Luke 11:4c for those areas of your life that are vulnerable.

DAY FIVE LESSON

Today we continue looking at Jesus' temptations—as well as our own. We have seen that His victory over temptation prepared Him for areas of His ministry.

Reread Luke 4:1-13.

18.What kind of response did Jesus give in every temptation? What does this teach you?

19.Read Ephesians 6:10-19 and answer these questions:

a. What part does God's word have in resisting
the enemy?

b. What other principles do you learn from this
metaphor of armor about your own spiritual
battles?

20.Often we are vulnerable to temptation when we stray
from "home." What principles of spiritual warfare do
you learn as you look at 1 Peter 5:5-11? Although every verse does not mention the enemy, that is the context and it covers many ways that we leave home and
become open to attack.

21.What parallels do you see in James 4:1-10?

22.**Sharing question:** Share with your group how one
temptation that you have overcome has helped prepare you to serve God and His people.

• **Diamonds in the Word:** Consider James 1:12-16.
How do you reconcile this with Jesus' experience and
with the Lord's Prayer in Luke 11:4? Write down the
explanation as you would give it to a new believer.

23.**Responding to God:** Considering the principles that
you saw in Ephesians, 1 Peter, and James, what spe-

cific action can you take to better stand against temptation? Write out a prayer asking for God's strength to follow through.

The story that follows is Deborah's true story of overcoming temptation by the power of God. I so appreciate the women who chose to share their struggles and temptations with you through this study. As you read these stories each week, think through how the principles of the lesson apply to the situation. I hope that you enjoy reading them as much as I did!

DEBORAH'S STORY (A CLASSMATE WITH WHOM I GREW UP WITH)

Although I came to faith at 13 in Galveston, Texas... some years after college I spent time playing by my own rules. After I prayed for spiritual direction, God surrounded me at work with Christians that were praying for me. I wasn't too concerned about what they thought of my relationships because their judgment would be on their head not mine. Then one day God made it abundantly clear to me that the relationship I had with this man I was seeing was wrong. I would have to give him up. It was difficult. I had an index card next to the phone that said, "No, I won't see you again."

When he called I read the card. When he would try to convince me otherwise I knew that he didn't understand what kind of spiritual relationship I had buried within my heart. It felt so good to be home spiritually. There were many unresolved issues but I had to believe that since the Father had not abandoned me he would take me the rest of the way home.

Fifteen years have passed. This fall I had an   opportunity to share with some women my journey. I wasn't proud of what I had done but was amazed by God's forgiveness and grace. I believe that sharing my experience opened the door for some women to share their burdens with me. They too are seeking God's will. I now pray for these women regularly. I consider it now a blessing to be able to share how patient and how far the Father will go to reach one of his own.

Coming Home to Jesus

Week Two—Leave it Behind and Come Home

A Precious Word from God

"And he got up and followed Him, leaving everything behind."

> Description of Matthew in Luke 5:28 (NET)

Introduction

When I go home, I have to leave behind the place where I am. Such is God's call for our lives—come home and leave everything else behind!

As we pick up Jesus' story we realize that His ministry had begun. His headquarters became the city of Capernaum in the area of Galilee, near His hometown of Nazareth is located. Luke divides his gospel geographically, and this Galilean ministry is covered in Luke 4:14-9:50.

Right from the start, people had differing responses to Jesus' ministry. Some things never change!

DAY ONE STUDY

Read Luke 4:14-30.

1. What was the primary message in Jesus' sermon in the synagogue in Nazareth?

2. What was Jesus' point to these people in using the examples of Elijah and Elisha?

3. How did the people respond and why? How might you have felt in their place?

- *Diamonds in the Word:* Look up the passage in Isaiah from which Jesus read. Explain how Jesus' ministry fulfilled the various aspects of this prophecy. Jesus did not quote the entire prophecy concerning the Messiah. What did He omit and why might He have chosen to do so?

4. Review the entire passage, and describe Jesus' early ministry in Galilee. Contrast the reception He received in His hometown of Nazareth with that elsewhere in the area.

5. *Sharing Question:* Describe a time in your life when you responded in anger to God's message to you. Why did you respond this way?

6. *Responding to God:* Are you struggling with God's message to you in any particular area of life right now? If so, share it with your group and make it your written prayer request this week.

Day Two Study

Read Luke 4:31-41.

7. What miracles did Jesus perform? What do you learn about Jesus' power and authority from them?

8. Compare Jesus' reception from the people in the synagogue in Capernaum with the response of those in Nazareth (yesterday's lesson).

9. What do you learn from these miracles that can help you when you are tempted to fear the power of evil?

- *Diamonds in the Word:* Jesus rebuked the demons to silence about His identity. Consider why He may have done this. Read at least two commentaries or notes in study Bibles. Then, write down your thoughts.

Read Luke 4:42-44.

10. What do you learn about Jesus' priorities from His response to the crowds?

11. How does Paul's statement in Gal. 1:10 compare with Jesus' response here?

12. *Sharing Question:* In what situations do you tend to please people rather than God? How do you discern what God wants you to do when there are other good, positive works that need to be done?

13.**Responding to God:** Write a prayer asking God for the wisdom and discernment to help you know the difference in good works and the best work— that which He has planned for you to do.

DAY THREE STUDY

Read Luke 5:1-11.

14. The disciples went out in the water twice to fish. Contrast the two situations, etc. What did the second trip out reveal about Jesus?

15. What do you learn from Simon Peter here that you can apply to your own relationship with Jesus?

• **Diamonds in the Word:** This was not Jesus' first encounter with Simon Peter. Look in an exhaustive concordance and find accounts of their previous interactions. Write down what you learn.

16. Compare the interaction between Jesus and Simon with these other situations of encounter with God. Write down the similarities you observe in the responses of these other men to Simon's:

   a. Isaiah 6:1-8

   b. Eze. 1:22-2:8

c. Acts 22:1-21.

In all of these situations the encounter with God involved a call to God's work.

17. Read these verses and write down some of what God calls us to do in our work for Him:

   a. 1 Peter 1:14-17

   b. 1 Peter 2:4, 5

   c. 1 Peter 2:9-12

18. **Sharing Question:** How are you doing at this point in your life with each of these areas of God's call? Be honest and specific.

19. **Responding to God:** Write a prayer or poem of confession and commitment based upon the verses you read in #17. If you prefer, draw a picture representing your response to God's call.

DAY FOUR STUDY

Read Luke 5:12-26.

20. Contrast the situations of the two sick men, including how they got to Jesus.

21. Why was it significant that Jesus forgave before He healed the second man? What was he claiming for Himself? What did the healing prove?

22. Compare the role of faith in these two healing situations.

- **Diamonds in the Word:** Begin to track various kinds of miracles throughout Jesus' ministry in Luke beginning in Luke 4:14, the commencement of His ministry. You might list them by type of miracle, *i.e.*, healing, casting out demons, or authority over nature. Note when Jesus healed and what part faith played.

23. Review Luke 4:42-44; 5:5-16. What do you learn from Jesus' example concerning busyness?

24. **Sharing Question:** In what ways are you, as a friend, similar to the men who carried their friends' stretcher? What is one specific way that you can be more like them?

25. **Responding to God:** Ask God for the grace to become the kind of friend these men were. Write down one specific way you will reach out to a friend in need this week, and share what happens with your group.

DAY FIVE STUDY

Read Luke 5:27, 28.

This new disciple is called Matthew in Matthew 9:9, 10. The *NET Bible* gives us insight into his two names.[3]

> Levi is likely a second name for Matthew because people often used alternative names in 1st century Jewish culture.
>
> NET Bible

We saw Simon Peter, James, and John leave everything and follow Jesus (Luke 5:9-11). Levi, or Matthew, is described as doing the same thing here. (In fact this is your *Precious Word from God* to memorize this week.)

26.*Sharing Question:* If you left everything behind to follow Jesus, what would that look like in your life today? What would have to change—your priorities, relationships, focus, job, etc.?

Read Luke 5:29-39.

The *NET Bible* gives us greater understanding of what it meant to be a tax collector in that day.[4]

> The tax collectors would bid to collect taxes for the Roman government and then add a surcharge, which they kept. Since tax collectors worked for Rome, they

---

[3] *NET Bible* Note 3, p. 1811
[4] *NET Bible* Note 9, p. 1802

were viewed as traitors to their own people and were not
well liked.

NET Bible

27. What criticisms did the Pharisees voice about Jesus?

- ***Diamonds in the Word***: "The marital imagery pictures God's relationship to His people in the Old Testament and in later Judaism (Is 54:5-6; 62:4-5; Jer
2:2; Ezek 16; Hos 2:14-23." [5] The New Testament pictures the Messiah as the bridegroom. Read Mt. 22:2;
25:1; Lk. 12:35-36; Eph. 5:22-33. How is the Messiah
like a bridegroom?

Read Luke 6:1-11.

28. How did Jesus anger the Pharisees through both
His healings and His defense of His actions?

Throughout this week's lesson we have seen people
respond to Jesus' message. Some were attracted to him
while others grew angry at His actions and His words.

29. Compare the responses of those you have studied
today. What would you say is the fundamental difference?

30. ***Sharing question:*** Have you responded to Jesus
as Levi and Peter did? What have you failed to
leave behind, that you are holding on to rather

---

[5] Darrell L. Bock, *Luke*, ed. Grand R. Osborne, The IVP New Testament Commentary Series, vol. 3 (Downers Grove, IL: InterVarsity Press, 1994), 110.

than release to Him? Why? How does that keep you from really coming home to Him?

31. ***Responding to God:*** Write a prayer or poem of confession and commitment to God. Ask for the grace to leave everything so that He can use you mightily for His kingdom.

32.

When I read Becky's story, I really could not believe how well it illustrated this lesson. Until she changed her attitude about leaving, she could not be at home.

BECKY'S STORY

After over 28 years of living in Austin, we were moving to Dallas. Glenn had been unemployed for six months, and had been offered a good job in Dallas. The timing seemed perfect. All our children were grown, the youngest having just graduated from high school and been accepted at the University of Texas. Our house in Austin was paid for, so we could afford to keep it for Ethan to live in while he was at UT. We joked that he was going to be at home, and his parents were going to come visit on weekends. Maybe we'd bring our laundry.

Dallas beckoned. It was an adventure. Glenn was from Mesquite, and his mother and sister still lived there. There was a great opportunity to get closer to them, especially since Glenn's sister was suffering from cancer. It seemed clear that Dallas was where God wanted us to be. We moved.

We found a great church right away. We got involved. I joined the women's Bible study, and both of us joined a Community group. I started going to treatments with Glenn's sister and mom. Glenn settled in to his job, enjoying the challenge, and the stimulation of a talented group of colleagues.

We went to Austin frequently on weekends, Maybe too frequently. It was good to see family and friends, but we hadn't been in Dallas long enough for it to feel like home, and Austin was becoming just a place to visit. I felt like I belonged nowhere. I was still sure that God wanted us in Dallas, but my head and my heart were not in the same place. I confessed my feeling to the community group, and they lifted me up in prayer.

As the year wore on, there were more trips to Austin. Our children were having problems. Ethan was struggling with school. Lynn's marriage was falling apart. She and her husband separated. My older daughter, Lorna, moved back into our house to save money. Her dog died. She had stress at work. It was hard to connect with James because his life was so busy. One weekend as we were returning to Dallas, I saw the city skyline in the distance, and I started crying. Glenn asked me what was wrong. I told him, "I don't want to be there. I just don't want to be in Dallas." But I knew that Dallas was where God wanted me to be. Where He wants me to be. I realized that I was resisting God's will. I was in Dallas, but I wasn't here with God. I confessed to Him my feelings and asked for strength to believe that He would take care of my family. I acknowledged that they belong to Him, and He loves them more than I do. Of course, I always knew those things are true, but the head and the heart had to come together.

Last time as we were returning from Austin, I again looked up at the skyline in the distance. But this time, my heart leapt. I was coming home; home to the place God wants me to be.

Coming Home to Jesus

Week Three—Be Humble and Come Home

A PRECIOUS WORD FROM GOD

"Blessed are you who are poor, for the kingdom of God belongs to you."

Jesus in Luke 6:20 (NET)

INTRODUCTION

Our study this week involves the stories of several people who were poor spiritually, realizing their total dependence upon God. As we think about what it means to come home to Jesus, we realize an attitude of humility is a prerequisite.

DAY ONE STUDY

Read Luke 6:12-16.

1. Review Luke 6:1-11. What was happening when Jesus chose the twelve?

2. What do you learn about making major decisions from Jesus?

3. Read John 6:64. We Christians often think that if we pray enough and ask God to open the right doors, all will go well; otherwise, we conclude that we must have missed God's will. What do we learn about this idea from this passage about Jesus' choosing of the twelve and this verse in John?

4. Read John 15:8, 16-17. What do these verses mean in a personal way to those of us who are disciples of Jesus?

• **Diamonds in the Word:** Look up the word "apostles" in a Greek dictionary. What was the significance of using that term for the twelve? What does it tell you about their ministries?

5. **Sharing question:** Relate a story from your life when you made a major decision with much prayer. As you look back, how do you see God's hand in that decision, even if things did not go smoothly or as you expected?

6. **Responding to God:** Write a prayer concerning a big or small decision that you are currently facing. Can you tell God that you will trust Him, believing

that He knows better than you, even when the results are not easy?

DAY TWO STUDY

Read Luke 6:17-49.

You may be more familiar with Matthew's account of this, or a similar sermon. Although Jesus stood on a plateau, or level place, it could have been in the midst of mountains; thus, this may be the same sermon recorded in more detail in Matthew 5-7, known as the Sermon on the Mount. If not, Jesus repeated some of the major teachings on another occasion. We could spend a long time on this message because the teaching is so rich. Sadly, we do not have enough time to do so. You might mark this spot and return to it once the entire study of Luke is over so you can study it in more detail.

Your *Precious Word from God* this week is from this lesson. As you memorize it, meditate upon what it means to be poor.

7. There are four contrasts in Luke 6:20-26. By saying it in both positive and negative ways, Jesus emphasized His point. Summarize the four contrasts.

8. List the specific ways Jesus taught us to love our enemies (6:27-36).

9. *Sharing question:* Think of the person who is your enemy by Jesus' definition—the one who hates you, mistreats you, strikes you, or steals from you. How are you doing with loving actions toward him or her? What one specific loving action can you do for her this week in application of Jesus' comments?

10. In light of the context of the entire passage (6:17-49), do Jesus' instructions against judging others mean that we cannot hold them accountable, calling their words or actions sinful, or determine they have a heart issue? Explain your answer.

- *Diamonds in the Word:* Use your exhaustive concordance to find other New Testament verses about judging others. How do you reconcile Luke 6:37 with the others?

11. *Sharing question:* Evaluate yourself according to Luke 6:43-49. How does this reflect humility? What can you do to listen and obey more carefully?

12. *Responding to God:* If you are artistic, draw a picture that represents some part of Jesus' message in this sermon. Put yourself in it to represent your response to that message. If are you not artis-

tic, try it anyway☺ You don't have to show it to anyone! Then, talk to God about it.

Day Three Study

Read Luke 7:1-10.

13. How did the centurion exhibit spiritual poverty
and faith?

14. What was Jesus' response to this faith and why?
What specific things can you learn about faith and
humility from the centurion's example?

Read Luke 7:11-17.

15. What were the results of Jesus' raising the widow's
son?

16. The centurion showed great faith, and Jesus responded. Why did Jesus act in the case of the widow, according to the text? What does this teach
you about Jesus' character?

- **Diamonds in the Word:** Some believe and teach
that faith always results in healing. Study Matt. 8:16-

17; Isaiah 53:5; 1 Peter 2:24, 25 and comment. Use the stories that you have read in Luke and other examples from Jesus' healing ministry as you explain the Scriptural perspective on physical healing.

17. **Sharing question:** What lessons can you apply from the two stories you have studied today when those around you need healing?

18. **Responding to God:** Write a prayer, poem, or psalm of thanksgiving to Jesus for who He is based upon these two stories.

DAY FOUR STUDY

Read Luke 7:18-35.

19. One of those who heard the report about Jesus (Luke 7:17) was John the Baptist. Compare John's question for Jesus (Luke 7:19) with previous statements he made in John 1:26-34. What change do you see? Read Luke 3:15-20. What has happened that might explain John's question to Jesus?

20. **Sharing question:** What kinds of events in your life have brought doubt when you previously had faith?

21. Compare Jesus' answer to John with His message in the synagogue in Nazareth (Luke 4:18-21).

22. *Sharing question:* How does Jesus' assessment of John the Baptist (Luke 7:24-35) despite John's doubt encourage you?

• *Diamonds in the Word:* Do a character study of John the Baptist. Use your exhaustive concordance and study every passage that mentions him. Write down what you learn about his character.

23. *Sharing question:* If Jesus evaluated you before others, what would He say? What do you want Him to say about you at the end of your life? What actions do you need to take to become that person? What part does humility play in being that person?

24. *Responding to God:* Write a prayer of self-assessment, and request God to change you into the person you just described.

DAY FIVE STUDY

Read Luke 7:36-50.

25. Describe the events at the Pharisee's dinner.

What was nard? The *NET Bible* tells us.[6]

Nard or spikenard is a fragrant oil from the root and spike of the nard plant of northern India. This perfumed oil, if made of something like nard, would have been extremely expensive, costing up to a year's pay for an average laborer.

NET Bible

26. Contrast the woman's love for Jesus with the Pharisee's.

- **Diamonds in the Word:** All of the gospels record a story of Jesus being anointed by a woman. Compare Matt. 26:6-13; Mark 14:3-9; and John 12:1-8 and this account in Luke. Which ones record the same story and which may be a completely different event. Why?

27. **Sharing question:** If your love for Jesus were measured by your sacrificial actions, how would you rate? What specific action would be most revealing? Why?

Read Luke 8:1-3.

Considering that this was the first century rather than our own, this is an amazing account. As women, we need to appreciate Luke for the stories of women that he alone of the gospel writers includes. It is interesting that there is no record in the gospels of a woman responding negatively to Jesus!

---

[6] *NET Bible* Note 18, p. 1820

28. What impresses you about these women, particularly considering their culture?

29. ***Sharing question:*** Think about the woman who anointed Jesus and these women who traveled with Him. In what one way would you like others to better see your love relationship with Jesus? What can you do to improve to make it true?

30. ***Responding to God:*** Just as Peter and Levi, or Matthew, left everything behind and followed Jesus, so did a group of women. Ask God to give you such love and commitment to Him.

In our lesson we saw Jesus move on behalf of those who lacked faith. This next story reminds us that God is at work for our benefit even when we doubt Him.

DOROTHY'S STORY

During the first year of our marriage God moved on my behalf when I did not have the faith to believe that He would. My mother died unexpectedly during that year. I was pregnant with our first child. We were living in a different city, and I knew no one. Dick had been working there for a year before we married. Even though I was a Christian and also had the assurance that my mother was with the Lord, I was still angry with God for taking my mother from me. It hurt so much knowing that our child would not grow up having a grandmother.

For several months I kept to myself, grieving quietly and making no effort to try to make new friends in my new town. God reached out to me through one particular family in the church we attended. Sam worked for the same company as Dick. His wife Sue wouldn't take no for an answer when I insisted that I didn't want a baby shower. I told her I had no friends there to invite. She invited her own friends, and they showered me with much love and support.

The Lord gave us a beautiful baby girl. Six months after she was born Dick was transferred back to Dallas. We still keep in touch with our friends there who reached out to us in our time of need.

Coming Home to Jesus

Week Four—Die to Self and Come Home

A PRECIOUS WORD FROM GOD

"If anyone wants to become my follower, he must deny himself, take up his cross daily, and follow me. For whoever wants to save his life will lose it, but whoever loses his life for my sake will save it."

Jesus in Luke 9:23-24 (NET)

INTRODUCTION

It seems that week after week Jesus' words in Luke confront us with the demands of being a Christ-follower. So far we have been asked to leave everything behind and to humble ourselves if we are to really come home to the peace and rest in Jesus. Now we see that we need to die to self. Although our salvation is not dependent upon how well we accomplish this, our blessing, our peace and our witness often are. It's not easy to get home sometimes

DAY ONE STUDY

Read Luke 8:4-15.

1. List the four kinds of ground described in this parable and Jesus' explanation of each.

2. What was Jesus' purpose in using parables? Is this what you previously understood? If not, what was your understanding?

- **Diamonds in the Word:** Some debate which soil(s) represent true salvation. Some would say that true believers can be barren while others say that they will produce fruit, but not always or all to the same extent. Read these cross-references and consider how they inform the debate: Phil. 1:6; Col. 1: 21-23; Jude 1:24; 1 John 2:19; and John 10:27-30. What is your perspective of this issue, and upon what verses do you base it?

   Read Luke 8:16-18.

3. What does the light of truth in Jesus do in our lives?

Read Luke 8:19-21.

4. Review Luke 5:33-39. Jesus brought changes to the old order of things. What kinds of changes are mentioned in Luke 8:19-21?

5. *Sharing question:* What is your relationship with Jesus according to His words in v. 21? How does this make you feel? What does that suggest about the kind of relationship you have with Him in a practical way? How does understanding this relationship affect your feeling of coming home to Jesus?

6. ***Responding to God:*** Write a prayer in which you talk honestly to God about your family, both your old physical family and your new spiritual family.

DAY TWO STUDY

Watch in your reading today for four miracles that Jesus performed.

Read Luke 8:22-55.

7. What were the four miracles and how did they differ?

8. Describe how each of these people who came into contact with Jesus reacted to the miracles:

Disciples in the boat:

Demon-possessed man:

Herdsmen:

People of the town:

Woman in the crowd:

Jairus and his wife:

9. What would you say is the primary component that causes people to react differently to Jesus?

10. *Sharing question:* How did you initially respond to the stories of Jesus? There is a journey to faith and we get there in different ways. Where are you in the journey?

- *Diamonds in the Word:* Continue to work on your list of miracles. Look in the other three gospels and read the accounts of these miracles there. What new information do you gain from those writers?

11. ***Responding to God:*** Ask God to open your heart to see Jesus' miracles as if you were watching them unfold before you. Worship at His feet.

DAY THREE STUDY

Read Luke 9:1-11.

12. Where did the twelve receive their power and authority? What surprises you about the instructions that Jesus gave them?

13. What do the following verses say about your power as a believer? What difference should that make to you each day?

    a. Acts 1:8

    b. Matt. 28:18-20

    c. John 15:5

d. 2 Timothy 1:7-8

Read Luke 9:12-27.

14. The reaction of the crowd to Jesus' feeding them is not recorded. Dr. Bock says that indicates that the lesson is primarily for the disciples.[7] What may they have learned for future ministry from this occasion?

15. Compare the disciples' answer about Jesus' identity with the news that confused Herod (9:7-9).

---

[7] Bock, 164.

16.What further understanding did Jesus feel that the disciples needed in order to be ready to proclaim Jesus as Israel's Messiah (9:21-22)? In other words, they weren't ready yet. Why would they need that information before they proclaimed Him?

The **_Precious Word from God_** this week is Luke 9:23-24. As you memorize it, meditate upon its ramifications in your life.

Understanding Jesus as the Christ (Messiah) means that we realize more and more what coming home to Him really means. The *NET Bible* helps us understand what the meaning of taking up the cross daily would have meant to the first century Jews.[8]

> Only Luke mentions taking up one's cross *daily*. To bear the cross means to accept the rejection of the world for turning to Jesus and following him. Discipleship involves a death that is like a crucifixion.
>
> NET Bible

17. Read Galatians 6:12-14. How do these verses help you understand the quote above?

- ***Diamonds in the Word:*** Compare Luke 9:23-26 with similar passages in the other gospels. Note to whom Jesus spoke and what He taught. Write down your understanding of Jesus' words.

---

[8] *NET Bible* Note 8, p. 1829

18.***Sharing question:*** Are you willing to not only die physically, if necessary, but also die to other things that help you better follow Jesus? How are you doing with giving up material things for the sake of the gospel? Have you been willing to share the gospel at the risk of rejection from friends, family, or co-workers?

19.***Responding to God:*** Talk to God about taking up your cross daily to follow Him as defined by the quote on the previous page. Write down what He says to you about what that looks like in your life in specific ways—in your job, your leisure, and your time.

DAY FOUR STUDY

Read Luke 9:28-36.

20. How did this event fulfill the prediction of 9:27?

21. What was the departure, or exodus, that Jesus was about to take (9:31)?

22. How were God's words in 9:35 a rebuke to Peter?

- ***Diamonds in the Word:*** Read in your commentaries or study Bible notes about this event, called the Transfiguration. Write down your thoughts and insights.

23. ***Sharing question:*** Have you ever been guilty of thinking of Jesus as being on the same level with you or other biblical characters? How? How did that affect your faith?

24. ***Sharing question:*** Read Moses' prayer in Exodus 33:18. Do you really have a heart to have God answer that prayer in your life? Why or why not?

25.***Responding to God:*** Write a prayer based upon Ex. 33:18 or a prayer asking God to give you the kind of love for Him that erupts in this prayer.

DAY FIVE STUDY

The disciples' mountaintop experience was closely followed by a failure of faith.

Read Luke 9:37-45.

26. Why might believers fall prey so easily to failure after a mountaintop type of experience with Jesus?

- **Diamonds in the Word:** Study passages in the four gospels where Jesus cast out demons. What do you learn about those who are demon-possessed? What do you learn about the cure?

Read Luke 9:46-50.

27. What do the events of the demon-possessed boy (vv. 37-43), Jesus' words (vv. 44-45), the disciples' argument (vv. 46-48), and John's words (vv. 49-50) reveal about where the disciples were spiritually at this point?

28. **Sharing question:** With which of the stories about the disciples do you identify most? Why?

29.**Sharing question:** Where are you today spiritually? What reactions have you had this past week that reveal your real heart?

30.**Sharing question:** How much allegiance do you show God? How willing are you to die for Him? How would you rate yourself on a scale of 1-10? Why?

31.**_Responding to God:_** Write a prayer or poem con-
fessing your struggles with self, faith, and spiritual
pride.

Like these disciples, Carrie experienced temptation after a mountaintop experience.

CARRIE'S STORY

I think about this summer when I went to Israel.
The whole trip was a mountain top experience! Minute
by minute I was surrounded by the truth of God's Word.
Scriptures were coming to life as I stood on the shore of
the Sea of Galilee, wondered in the wilderness, and
walked the narrow streets of Jerusalem. However, there
was one point during the trip, when we were in the
ancient city of Dan (where the tribe of Dan settled) when
I was tempted with disillusion. Satan was whispering to
me that the bible was not real, it was all made up. He
wanted me to believe that all of this land and places
mentioned in the bible were written and made-up sto-

ries by man and not inspired by God. The experience in Israel was so overwhelming emotionally, that I for one minute thought "this is too good to be true."

I prayed to the Lord at that moment, while walking in the ancient city of Dan, to take these thoughts of doubt from me. I didn't want them and I wished I weren't having them. I asked for his forgiveness for entertaining those thoughts and acknowledged His goodness, His faithfulness and His power to be creator of all. The Holy Spirit then reminded me of His authority, His miracles and His truth.

God was faithful and good to me to help me through my temptation when I called upon His name. Each time I begin to doubt and buy into Satan's deception, I remember my Israel experience and call upon His name.

Coming Home to Jesus

Week Five—Come Home but Don't Turn Back

A Precious Word from God

> "No one who puts his hand to the plow and looks back is fit for the kingdom of God."
>
> Jesus in Luke 9:62 (NET)

Introduction

This week we move into a new section of the book of Luke. We looked at the time of Jesus' birth and preparation and then His ministry in Galilee. Luke 9:51 rec-

61

ords the beginning of Jesus' final journey to Jerusalem, where He would be tortured, killed, buried and exalted. As recorded in Luke, it is not a straight line trip from Galilee to Jerusalem, but it is "a journey of destiny in which Jesus must meet His fate (Lk 13:31-15)."[9]

Go with Jesus as He takes His final journey. Learn from Him how to face life as He faced death.

DAY ONE STUDY

Read Luke 9:51-56.

There are several translations of the Greek words for Jesus' actions in v. 51. The NASB reads, "He was determined." The NIV says, "Jesus resolutely set out." The NET is similar: "Jesus set out resolutely."

1. What understanding of Jesus' attitudes or feelings do these words give you in the light of what He knew awaited Him in Jerusalem?

---

[9] Bock, 179.

2. Jesus faced rejection all along this journey. What reason is given for the Samaritan's attitude toward Jesus' visit (v53)?

3. How did James and John react to the Samaritans? What did this reveal about their hearts?

- *Diamonds in the Word:* Read 2 Kings 1. Why might James and John have seen their situation with the Samaritans as similar to this one faced by Elijah?

Read Luke 9:57-62. The *Precious Word from God* is from this passage.

4. Considering Jesus' responses to the three men who said they wanted to follow Him, what was He teaching about being His disciple?

5. Compare the attitudes of these three men to Jesus' attitude in 9:51.

6. **Sharing question**: If someone were to look at the way you spend your time and your money, what priorities would they assign to your life? Why?

7. ***Responding to God:*** Confess the ways that you are like these three men. Recommit to follow Jesus and all that means, setting out resolutely as He did to what awaited Him.

DAY TWO STUDY

Read Luke 10:1-16.

8. What did Jesus say that explained the seriousness of rejecting His messengers?

9. We are all called to be workers in the harvest, and the Bible gives us much instruction for that role.

Consider what instructions for the workers are given in these few verses:

    a. Matt. 28:18-20

    b. Phil. 2:14-15

    c. 1 Peter 4:11

    d. 1 Peter 3:1-4

10. *Sharing question:* How are you doing with Jesus' specific instructions to you as a worker in the harvest? Have you "put your hand to the plow" in reality? Why or why not?

- *Diamonds in the Word:* Spend some time thinking through other verses with which you are familiar, verses that give you instructions as to how to live before others so that you draw them to Jesus. Write down those that come to your mind. How are you doing with them?

Read Luke 10:17-24.

11. How were the disciples blessed more than prophets and kings? Explain Jesus' words.

12. *Sharing question:* What advantages do you have in the United States and in your specific life situation that may bring you a stricter judgment than believers elsewhere?

Dr. Tim Sykes

13.***Responding to God:*** Ask God to show you how to use those advantages for His glory. Listen for His voice and write down what He says to you. Resolutely set out to do what He tells you, rather than turn back from the work.

DAY THREE STUDY

Most of you will already be familiar with Jesus' parable.

Read Luke 10:25-37.

14.Describe the conversation that led to the parable.

The Jews of that day would have considered the Samaritan a traitor or at least a "bad guy", but Jesus made him the hero of the story.

15. Contrast the attitudes of the lawyer (vv. 25-29) and the Samaritan.

16. Parables are stories with one main teaching. Write a one sentence statement of Jesus' point in this story.

• **Diamonds in the Word:** Use your biblical reference material to look up parables. What are they? What is their purpose? How are they to be interpreted? What insights do you receive that help you better understand this particular parable?

17. According to these verses how did Jesus model loving a neighbor?

a. Rom. 5:6-8

b. Phil. 2:5-8

c. 1 Peter 2:21-25

18. *Sharing question:* Who is the one person or type
of person who is most difficult for you to treat as
your neighbor? Why? If you were the Samaritan
and that person were the injured party, how would
you have felt and what would you have done? (Be
honest!)

19.**Responding to God**: Ask God to show you one specific way to love this person as yourself. Write down what you will do in the first person (I will . . .). Set out resolutely to do it! Be prepared to share your answer with your group.

DAY FOUR STUDY

The story of Mary and Martha is another golden nugget about women in this gospel. I so appreciate Luke's giving us a better perspective of Jesus' relationship with women! You may have heard and read this story to the point of annoyance. As you read it again, try to picture yourself right there in Martha's house.

Read Luke 10:38-42.

20. Contrast Mary and Martha's priorities.

- **Diamonds in the Word:** Read in your Bible notes or commentaries to learn more about women's situations in that era.

21. Did Jesus devalue Martha's service? Explain your answer.

22.***Sharing question:*** In what ways are you serving Jesus? Why are you serving in those specific ways? For recognition? From guilt? Out of obedience? For its joy? Other motivations or combinations?

23.***Sharing question:*** Make a list of the things in your life that distract you from time with God.

24.***Responding to God:*** Pray over the list you made, writing down your thoughts about changes you need to make. Then, resolutely set out to do them, just as Jesus did. If you desire, write it as your weekly prayer request.

DAY FIVE STUDY

Read Luke 11:1-13.

Not only does Luke emphasize women in his gospel, but he also emphasizes prayer. We cannot truly come home to Jesus if we don't take part in the hard work of prayer. The particular prayer Jesus prayed in this passage is usually called The Lord's Prayer, but a more appropriate name may be The Disciple's Prayer.[10]

---

[10] *NET Bible* Note 29, p. 1836.

25.In light of Jesus' purpose in giving the prayer, why may that be a more appropriate name? What was Jesus doing when the disciple approached Him?

Many times we learn to pray with a pattern. We may pray in the order of ACTS (adoration, confession, thanksgiving, and supplication). Personally I like the PRAY pattern (praise, repent, ask, yield).

26.Do you see any pattern in Jesus' prayer in topics and/or order? What insights do you have into prayer from this model prayer?

27.What lessons on prayer did Jesus teach in vv. 5-10?

28.Compare James 1:17 with Luke 11:11-13. When God answers "no" to our prayers, what may the reason be according to these verses?

- *Diamonds in the Word:* Compare Matt. 6:5-15 with this passage in Luke. What additional lessons on prayer do you learn from Matthew?

29.*Sharing question:* What prayer request have you been praying persistently for the longest period of time? What has been difficult about continuing to pray?

30.*Responding to God:* Pray for the grace to set out resolutely to work hard in prayer for the things that you know are His will and His good gifts. Pray for the wisdom to know the difference.

TINA'S STORY

The summer of 2001 was full of life changing events. I married John, my friend of almost seven years, moved to Dallas for the first time, got a new corporate job, and sent my new husband off to medical school. Things seemed so hopeful and wonderful for us both and I do not hesitate to say that my whole life was wrapped up in John. I had been very faithful to my relationship with God in college and was very involved with my church there as a leader. But at some point during our wedding, I unconsciously (and incorrectly) decided to make John "lord of my life." Nothing could have been more crushing, as I would soon find out. Medical school proved to be far more challenging and time consuming than either of us ever expected, and because he is human and fallible, John was not always there for me. I felt so alone in this new, huge city, with no really good friends and no church home. I made many mistakes trying to deal with this, but I finally realized that the root of my troubles lied in my priorities, and where I had put my faith. I kept trying to lean on John and when he wasn't there for me, I turned to worse and worse alternatives. If I had only leaned on God and trusted in Him, I know He would have been there for me in every way. God never lets us down, even if things are in His timing, He is ALWAYS there for us. But we have to rely on Him, put Him first, and seek Him. Fortunately, even when we don't, He comes after us. During the summer of 2002 I forced myself to go to the Women's Bible study at my church. Not only did God wrap His arms around me, but He put godly women in my life that are still in my study today. It's still a daily, conscious struggle to put God first, but I have felt the consequences in my life and relationships when I don't. There is no doubt in my mind that putting God first in my life increases both my joy in happy times and my strength during difficult times.

Coming Home to Jesus

Week Six—Give it Up and Come Home

A PRECIOUS WORD FROM GOD

"For where your treasure is, there your heart will be also."

Jesus in Luke 12:34 (NET)

INTRODUCTION

It feels like every lesson hits me right in the face and I land on the floor! Over and over Jesus tells us that coming home to Him involves changing a lot of our attitudes and actions. He calls us to give Him more than we have ever given Him before. He calls us to come home with our whole hearts.

This week our study deals with a lot of subjects. We cannot cover it all in detail but will have to focus on certain verses. If you have time, you might look at the **Diamonds in the Word** optional study questions to give you more insight into those passages.

DAY ONE STUDY

Read Luke 11:14-32.

1. What were the various responses to Jesus' casting out the demon (11:14-16)?

2. How did Jesus argue the absurdity of the accusation in 11:15? Explain His logic in your own words.

3. According to 11:16 a group tested Jesus. How did Jesus rebuke them later in the passage? What is ironic, given what Jesus just did? What does it reveal about them?

• ***Diamonds in the Word:*** Read the notes in your Bible or commentary concerning the illustration Jesus gave in 11:21-26. Explain them in your own words.

Jesus was hard on those who looked for signs because they did not believe what they had already seen. He was the only sign they needed.

4. ***Sharing Question:*** Have you ever been guilty of asking for signs before you were willing to risk belief? In what situation right now are you afraid to

step out in faith unless you see the "sign" first? It may be things such as a career path, a step forward in a dating relationship, witnessing to a co-worker, or risking vulnerability in your small group.

5. Compare Luke 11:27-28 with Luke 8:19-21. What truth did Jesus continue to emphasize? Why might He have done this?

6. *Responding to God:* Consider your answers to #4 and #5. What response do you need to make to Jesus' teaching? Write down your prayer.

DAY TWO STUDY

Read Luke 11:33-54.

Jesus' illustration in 11:33-36 pictured the attitude of the Pharisees that we see revealed in the remainder of this passage.

7. How did this illustration set the stage for Jesus' words to the Pharisees in 11:37-54?

8. Go back through the passage and list the various attitudes and actions of the Pharisees and lawyers (experts in the law) that Jesus denounces.

The Pharisees had a choice at this point—to open their hearts and come home to God or to refuse to hear God's word and repent. They chose the latter.

9. How did their choice affect their interaction with Jesus (11:53-54)?

- *Diamonds in the Word:* Go to your Bible resources such as a Bible dictionary, a Bible encyclopedia, or a commentary and find out more about the Pharisees and scribes.

Read Luke 12:1-12.

10.In light of the Pharisees' power and influence in the land and their obvious distaste for Jesus, how did Jesus both warn and encourage the disciples?

11. **Sharing question:** What did Jesus say here that encourages you as you face a specific fear?

12.**Responding to God:** Write a prayer or poem of thanksgiving to God for the truths and promises in His Word.

Day Three Study

Today's lesson involves a lot of verses, but persevere because tomorrow you will cover only seventeen verses! It all averages out.

Read 12:13-34. Memorize the **Precious Word from God** this week, and meditate upon its meaning for you personally.

13. We live in a highly materialistic society. Summarize the major principles Jesus taught about material goods in these verses.

14.***Sharing question:*** Go to your closet and consider what is there. How does it reveal where you are really at home, in this world or in heaven?

Read Luke 12:35-59.

15. How do these verses relate to Jesus' teaching on treasure?

16.***Sharing question:*** When Jesus returns, we will stand before Him and account for our lives, not to pay for our sins but to gain reward. Share with your group how much this truth affects you as you live daily. Using the illustrations of the parables, which kind of slave/servant are you?

- **Diamonds in the Word:** Explain the relationship of 12:49-59 to this section or do further study of the bema seat judgment in 2 Cor. 5:9-10.

17. **Sharing question:** Review Jesus' words in 12:30-34. Ask God to show you what you need to do with some of your "stuff" in order to come home with your full heart. Be specific.

18. **Responding to God:** Ask God to help you keep your eyes on the eternal rather than today's circumstances or the things that this world considers to be "needs".

DAY FOUR STUDY

Read Luke 13:1-9.

19. How did the Galileans' words reflect their beliefs about God as Judge (review Luke 12:57-59)? What was wrong with their perspective, according to Jesus?

20. How does the parable in Luke 13:6-9 relate to what Jesus said in 13:2-5? What was His main point in this parable?

- **Diamonds in the Word:** How would you explain the suffering in this world to someone who has just encountered tragedy? You are free to read on this subject. Use Scripture, even if you would not use it with the person.

Read Luke 13:10-17.

21. Contrast the responses of the synagogue official, the crowds, and Jesus' adversaries to all that happened in the synagogue.

22.**Sharing question:** What kinds of legalistic attitudes have you encountered from believers? Share
any attitudes of your own that reflect more concern with rules than with people.

23.How would you have felt, if you were this woman
at these points in the story:

- Before the healing

- After being healed

- Upon hearing the criticisms of the official

- After Jesus responded

24. **Sharing question:** Relate the story of a time when either you spoke up for "justice" or someone spoke up for you when you faced injustice.

25. **Responding to God:** Write a prayer asking God to give you Jesus' courage in facing the suffering and injustice of others. What do you have to give up in order to stand up for the rights of others? Is there any present situation in which you need to act?

DAY FIVE STUDY

Read Luke 13:18-30.

* ***Diamonds in the Word:*** Read the notes in your study Bible or commentary concerning the two parables in 13:18-20. How do they picture God's kingdom?

Jesus never answered the man's question of 13:23. Rather than talk about the few or the many, Jesus made the man focus on himself.

26. What did Jesus want this man to consider about himself (13:24-30)?

27. What relationship do you see between Jesus' words about the door in 13:24-25 and His teaching in 13:1-9?

28. *Sharing question:* It is so easy to turn our attention from our own relationship with God to others. We hear a sermon and think about a friend or co-worker who needs to hear it. We study for our weekly lesson in Luke and wish a family member

could be there to hear the discussion. Have you been guilty of failing to let God speak to you during this course by concerning yourself with others? Confess your attitude to your group. You may want to write down a prayer request for the week asking for your heart to be open to hear God's personal message for you so that you come home to Him.

Read Luke 13:31-35.

29.What surprises you from a human perspective about Jesus' attitude toward Jerusalem?

30.*Sharing question:* Do you grieve over those who will perish because they refuse to hear God's word? What about those who are the enemies of

Christ, who harm God's servants? Think of a person or group in this category—perhaps those in the bondage of Islam who hate Christians; perhaps Americans who fight for restrictions of our religious liberty. What did Jesus say about your attitude toward them in Luke 6:27-36?

31.*Responding to God:* Write a prayer for those you mentioned in the previous question. What attitudes do you have to give up to pray for them?

This woman literally came home by giving up her security and trusting God. She chose to invest in her family rather than in financial security. Consider in what sense you will come home when you trust God in a specific situation.

KAY'S H'S STORY

Kevin and I had always planned on my staying home once we had children. However, when the time came and Emily was born, it was more difficult than I had expected to leave a career I had worked so hard at for over 10 1/2 years. We had prayed, and planned, and sought advice from godly couples, and we believed we knew what God wanted us to do. However, giving up half our income while at the same time adding all the expenses of a new baby made me nervous. In the end, we decided just to trust God to provide for our needs, convinced of the importance of my investing time and energy in our child (and eventually children). The difficult thing to give up was not so much the money or the material things, though we have had to make different choices on spending than we would have if I had continued working. Really, it was much more difficult to give up the sense of control over our financial security and to trust God to take care of us.

We (mostly I) wrestled with this decision to leave work for several weeks after Emily was born. When I finally yielded completely to God, and with Kevin's encouragement, I went to the office one last time to tell my boss what we had decided. It also happens that he was Kevin's boss, too, and he was not surprised by our decision. In fact, he was very kind and wholeheartedly supported us. My resignation would take effect as soon as my maternity leave ended. But what came next is what really caused our faith and dependence in the Lord to deepen. About a week after I announced my decision to resign, I got a phone call from the project staffing administrator. He said the company was planning a "reduction in force" and, knowing that I had already planned to resign, he asked if I would like to volunteer for the lay-off. He explained the pros (several additional months of pay and benefits) and cons (there weren't any, since I was planning to leave anyway), and I told him Kevin and I would discuss it and get back to him. As Kevin and I talked later that day, we both realized that this was God's way of affirming our decision to trust Him with our finances and needs. It was like a huge sign saying, "I'll take care of it." And, through everything, He has.

Sometimes I get frustrated that we don't have the financial freedom two incomes would afford us, or the sense of security having both of us employed during such uncertain times might provide. But then I remember God's confirmation 6 1/2 years ago that investing in our children's eternal lives on a day-to-day basis is much more important right now than the material things we've given up, and I'm encouraged to keep trusting Him to provide.

Coming Home to Jesus

Week Seven—Be Faithful and Come Home

A PRECIOUS WORD FROM GOD

"The one who is faithful in a very little is also faithful in much, and the one who is dishonest in a very little is also dishonest in much. If then you haven't been trustworthy in handling worldly wealth, who will entrust you with the true riches?"

Jesus in Luke 16:10-11 (NET)

INTRODUCTION

As I have worked with believers through the years, I have found faithfulness to be in short supply. Many women volunteer and then fail to follow through with their responsibilities. Sometimes they even back out of promises they have made. Some women seek positions of authority; yet, they have failed to be faithful in lesser jobs.

As you study this lesson, ask God to reveal your résumé of faithfulness to you.

DAY ONE STUDY

Read Luke 14:1-14.

Again, Jesus healed on a Sabbath, but this time He took the initiative rather than waiting for criticism.

1. Describe what happened.

2. What is Jesus' point in the parable of 14:7-11? How does it apply to us in the church today?

3. What motivated the host according to 14:12? What would he have received if he had invited those who could not reciprocate?

4. *Sharing question:* Write down what you give others and what you do for them. Are you motivated by getting something back, perhaps friendship, praise, promotion or invitations? Ask God to reveal your true motives and admit them to your group.

Read Luke 14:15-24.

The comment of the guest in 14:15 elicits Jesus' parable. The *Net Bible* helps us understand the cultural significance of the parable.[11]

> To make excuses and cancel at this point was an insult in the culture of the time. Regardless of customs concerning responses to invitations, refusal at this point was rude.
>
> NET Bible

5. What unspoken misunderstanding about those who will participate in God's kingdom did Jesus correct through this story? What did lack of faithfulness reveal about the first group?

---

[11] *NET Bible* Note 10, p. 1851.

- *Diamonds in the Word:* Compare Romans 11:13-36 to this parable in Luke.

6. *Responding to God:* Write a prayer asking God to give you His heart for those on the fringes of society.

DAY TWO STUDY

Read Luke 14:25-35.

7. What did Jesus teach the multitudes about allegiance to Him?

Dr. Bock explains the idea of hate:[12]

"Hate" is used figuratively and suggests a priority of relationship. Jesus is first.

Dr. Darrell Bock in *Luke*

- ***Diamonds in the Word:*** What stories of God's people reveal this kind of allegiance? It may be a story from the Bible or one from the present day. How could you use it to illustrate Jesus' principle of allegiance to Him?

8. ***Sharing question:*** Before God, consider your call as Jesus' disciple. Think through your own relationships and possessions. Where is your alle-

_____

[12] Bock, 254.

giance in truth? You might write a prayer request to share with your group based on what God reveals to you about this.

9. What was Jesus' point in the parables of the tower and the battle? How does it relate to allegiance to Him?

10. How does the illustration of the salt relate to this context?

11. **Sharing question:** What possible costs in your life may come with total allegiance to Jesus? Be specific.

12.**Responding to God:** Write a prayer or poem asking God for the grace you need to truly live with Jesus as your first allegiance.

DAY THREE STUDY

Jesus told three stories but so related them that Luke calls them "this parable", as if it were one story (15:3).

- *Diamonds in the Word:* Find a source that lists all of the parables of Jesus. Which of those we have studied are unique to Luke and which are retold in other gospels? How do these particular ones relate to Luke's purpose in writing (1:1-4)?

  Read Luke 15:1-32.

13. What precipitated the telling of these stories (15:1-2)?

14. What is Jesus' central teaching common to all three of these stories?

15. How do these stories rebuke the Pharisees and their complaints against Jesus?

16. The third story is often referred to as the parable of the "Prodigal Son." Evaluate Jesus' points in this parable. Where is His emphasis—on the second son or somewhere else? If the title reflects the main story, what would you name it? Why?

17. **Sharing question:** Compare what happened to the younger son to your own story of salvation through God's grace that reached out to you as a sinner and of your coming home in response.

18. **Responding to God:** Write a prayer or poem of thanks to God for His mercies in forgiving you and in protecting you at times from the consequences you deserve. Thank Him for loving you so much that you drew you home with His love.

DAY FOUR STUDY

Read Luke 16:1-15.

Dr. Bock comments:[13]

This parable is probably the most difficult in Luke. Its point is clear enough—be generous and responsible with your resources—but how it makes the point is much discussed.

Darrell Bock in *Luke*

It is likely that the parable itself ends after the first part of v. 8, followed by Jesus' comments.[14]

19. What did Jesus commend about the manager or steward in the story?

---

[13] Bock, 262.
[14] NET Bible Note 37, p. 1855-1856.

20.Explain Jesus' lesson about using money in 16:9.

- **Diamonds in the Word:** Read two or more commentaries or notes in study Bibles about this parable. What insights do you gain?

21.What does financial faithfulness reveal about us (vv. 10-15)?

22.**Sharing question:** Read these verses and write down other areas where you are entrusted by God as a manager or steward. Evaluate your faithfulness in each area:

a. 1 Peter 4:10-11

b. 1 Cor. 4:1-5

The following verses relate to specific groups of people, elders or apostles; yet, we can learn lessons about stewardship from them. Write down your insights from each Scripture and again, evaluate your faithfulness:

a. Titus 1:7

b. 1 Cor. 9:16-17

Read Luke 16:16-18.

The last part of v. 16 is apparently difficult to translate. Dr. Bock makes this comment:[15]

> Most versions read *everyone is forcing his way into it* (NIV; NRSV has the variation

---

[15] Bock, 268-269.

"everyone tries to enter it by force"), but such as statement is manifestly not true. Everyone is not in a rush to enter in; many choose to reject the kingdom utterly. The key here is the Greek term *biazo*, which means "to apply force." But the voice of the verb is ambiguous in Greek. . . I would argue . . . that Jesus is speaking of the persuasion applied to all through preaching. . . The preaching of the good news offers the opportunity to enter into kingdom benefits. Through this message all are urged to enter in. The time of fulfillment has come, and all are asked to share in its blessing. But to do so one must hear Jesus, not scoff at his authority.

Darrell Bock in *Luke*

23. Jesus' comments in these verses seem disconnected to what He just said about financial faithfulness. Meditate upon the relationship between the two, and write down your insights.

24. ***Responding to God:*** Ask God to show you where you have fallen short in faithfulness and repent of those actions. Pray for the grace to become a wom-

an who is faithful to her word in every area of life, both large and small.

DAY FIVE STUDY

Read Luke 16:19-31.

25.Contrast Lazarus and the rich man.

26.**Sharing question:** Consider your lifestyle and your concern for the poor. How are you like the rich man? What are you doing to reach out to the poor?

27.What were the rich man's two requests of Abraham? What did he hope to accomplish?

28.How is the answer to the second request significant?

- **_Diamonds in the Word:_** Again, read what your commentary or study Bible says about this story. What do you learn?

29. How does this story relate to all Jesus has said from 14:7 on?

30. **_Responding to God:_** Write a prayer asking God for wisdom as you consider how you are to reach out to the poor around you. Write down the thoughts that He gives you. What should you do about those who beg at the street corners, etc.?

Dakan shares her story of how God gave her more and more ministry opportunities when she proved faithful in the small things.

DAKAN'S STORY

When our family relocated to California in 1994 I believed in my head that God had great things for us, but my heart was aching from being taken away from family and "home". We began attending a small church. I volunteered to assist the teacher of the 6th grade girls Sunday school class only to get to know the girls my daughter would be attending school with. My reasons were selfish for stepping forward. One month into the class the lead teacher became ill and could not return to teach, therefore I had become the lead teacher – not what I had signed up for! However God blessed me with those young girls and that experience. Months later the director of MOPS, Donna, asked me to speak at one of their meetings of 100 women, I laughed out loud – "Are you kidding," I said, "I am just now comfortable speaking to these 6th graders!" I declined, but driving home I thought maybe I should pull something together just in case she was persistent. I began to write out my testimony, finished it and put it away. More months passed and I was so relieved that Donna hadn't mentioned MOPS again. Then one night she called to ask if I would consider being the TITUS woman for MOPS and without hesitation, I said yes. At that very moment I asked myself where that came from, only months earlier I had declined to speak to the women as a one time event, and now I was committing to speak twice a month for 8 months.

I did not see it then but it is so clear to me now that all along the way the Lord was preparing me; knocking off more rough edges and refining me along the way in order to glorify Him. He was asking me to step out, trust what He could do with me and allow me to see the need I had for Him. In spite of my initial selfish motive, God demonstrated His love for me, His desire for my personal growth and the joy I received from following Him on a deeper level.

Coming Home to Jesus

Week Eight—Come Home; Jesus is Looking for You

A PRECIOUS WORD FROM GOD

"For the Son of Man came to seek and to save the lost."

Jesus
in Luke 19:10 (NET)

INTRODUCTION

Jesus was on a mission when He became a man; he had the Father's work to do. If we are to come home to Him, we must come in humility trusting that He must seek and save us for we are incapable of doing it ourselves. Consider what a sacrifice it was for Him to leave the grandeur of heaven, where everything praised Him, to come to earth to be ridiculed and rejected by those He came to save.

DAY ONE STUDY

Read Luke 17:1-6.

These verses contain some instructions for Christ-followers; we have responsibilities toward one another as part of the family of faith. Jesus emphasizes His words by saying, "Watch yourselves" (NET & NIV), or "Be on your guard" (NASB).

1. What makes these particular instructions so important that He would use these words?

2. How do these instructions relate to one another?

Sometimes understanding something about nature is helpful in understanding the Bible, as we see from this comment in the *NET Bible*.[16]

A black mulberry tree is a deciduous fruit tree that grows about 20 ft (6 m) tall and has black juicy berries. This tree has an extensive root system, so to pull it up would be a major operation.

NET Bible

3. ***Sharing question:*** Apparently, the disciples needed more faith to live this way. In what area of life do you need more faith if you are to live as Jesus desires you to live? Why?

Read Luke 17:7-10.

---

16 *NET Bible* Note 14, p. 1858.

4. Write a sentence explaining the point of this parable and how it applies to you personally.

Read Luke 17:11-19.

Again, Luke reminds us that these events all took place during the Jerusalem journey.

5. Describe the Samaritan leper's worship.

- **_Diamonds in the Word_**: Use your concordance to find all the instances where Jesus healed lepers. Compare His methods. Write down your thoughts and comments. Study the laws on leprosy in the Old Testament. What strikes you as important about Jesus' healing of the lepers?

6. ***Responding to God:*** Spend your remaining time with God, simply thanking Him for all His blessings. List as many as you can.

DAY TWO STUDY

Read Luke 17:20-21.

The NET Bible and the NASB read, "The kingdom of God is in your midst," while the NIV says, "within you." This explanation in the NET Bible helps explain the meaning.[17]

> [In your midst] is a far better translation than "in you." Jesus would never tell the hostile Pharisees that the kingdom was inside them. The reference is to Jesus present in their midst. He brings the kingdom. Another possible translation would be "in your grasp."
>
> Note #27 in NET Bible p. 1859

I find that there are times when I look around at the world trying to find God at work, to see signs of His kingdom program. Yet, often it is in His daily presence, His handiwork in my heart where I best see His reign advancing. He is preparing me to be part of His kingdom by making me a woman whose heart belongs to the King.

7. *Sharing question:* How has God revealed Himself to you this past week? How have you seen His kingdom in the midst of your daily life?

---

[17] *NET Bible* Note 27, p. 1859.

Read Luke 17:22-37.

Jesus' reference to the days of the Son of Man may be confusing, but the *NET Bible* explains:[18]

> This is a reference to the *days* of the full manifestation of Jesus' power in a fully established kingdom.

> NET Bible

8. What apparent misunderstanding about those days does Jesus correct in 17:23-24?

- ***Diamonds in the Word:*** This is Jesus' fifth prediction of His passion recorded in Luke. Go back and find the other references and note their contexts.

9. How were the days of Noah and Lot like the coming days of the Son of Man?

---

[18] *NET Bible* Note 29, p. 1859.

The time will come when judgment falls upon the earth. It may be a difficult concept for us to grasp. Yet, deep in our souls we long for justice as we look around at the evil and injustice that permeate our world. Peter describes the coming Day of Judgment in his second letter.

Read 2 Peter 3:7-13.

10. What do you learn from these verses about God's heart toward those facing judgment?

11. Rather than judgment, believers anticipate the fulfillment of God's promises. What awaits us according to 2 Peter 3:13?

12. **Responding to God:** Pray for those you know who need to come to faith, those whom God seeks to come home.

DAY THREE STUDY

Read Luke 18:1-8.

13. Luke explains the point of the parable himself. What is it (v.1)?

14. ***Sharing question:*** How does this parable en-
    courage you with a specific prayer need that you
    have right now?

Read Luke 18:9-14.

15. What quality is essential if we are to come home to
    Jesus according to this parable? Why must we
    have it when approaching God?

16. Too often we believers look down on unbelievers,
    or less "spiritual" believers, just as this Pharisee
    did. ***Sharing question:*** Do you tend to be proud
    of some of your behavior? Be honest about the ar-
    eas of pride in your heart—perhaps your service to
    God, your prayer life, your church attendance,

your success at work, your intelligence, or your abilities.

- ***Diamonds in the Word:*** Use your concordance to find other references to pride. Look up those that seem to relate. Write down any insights that you have.

Read Luke 18:15-17.

17. Explain how we can receive the kingdom like a child. What is it about a child that we must emulate? How does this relate to the parable of 18:9-14?

Read Luke 18:18-30.

We have read previously of Jesus dealing with money and possessions in His teaching. Review Luke 12:22-34.

18.Jesus put His finger on the rich man's sin. In the light of Luke 12:34, how would you describe it?

19.**Responding to God:** Come before the Father in confession today. Perhaps you need to be cleansed of pride, of thinking that you are a pretty good person. Maybe you need to confess that your heart is not fully His. Believe that He hears and will forgive (1 John 1:9).

DAY FOUR STUDY

Read Luke 18:31-34.

20. List all the things that Jesus predicted would happen to Him in Jerusalem.

Dr. Tim Sykes

This note in the *NET Bible* was very helpful in explaining why the disciples seem so dense![19]

> This failure of the Twelve to *grasp what Jesus meant* probably does not mean that they did not understand linguistically what Jesus said, but that they could not comprehend how this could happen to him, if he was really God's agent. The saying being *hidden* probably refers to God's sovereign timing.
>
> NET Bible

Read Luke 18:35-43.

21. How did the blind man reveal humility? What were the results?

Read Luke 19:1-10.

22. How did Zaccheus show humility?

---

[19] *NET Bible* Note 23, p. 1863.

Our ***Precious Word from God*** this week is 19:10, where Jesus states His earthly mission. As we think about coming home to Jesus, we need to remember that He seeks us even before we turn back home.

23.***Sharing question:*** How have you seen Jesus seek you at a time when you were lost, either as an unbeliever or as a stray sheep?

24.How does Romans 3:10-18 confirm the need for God to seek the unbeliever first?

- ***Diamonds in the Word:*** Study your commentaries on the Romans passage or your Bible encyclopedia concerning the depravity of man. Explain this concept in your own words.

25.***Responding to God:*** Write a prayer thanking God that He initiates our relationship; He does not wait for us to look for Him.

DAY FIVE STUDY

Read Luke 19:11-27.

26.Again, Luke comments on the reasons Jesus told a parable. Explain his words and how the parable relates to the situation.

27. With each character in the story below, describe three things: 1. their actions, 2. the nobleman's re-actions to those actions, and 3. what this reveals about their character:

Citizens—

Slave #1—

Slave #2—

Other slave—

28.***Sharing question:*** If Jesus returned today to claim the earth as His kingdom, how would you explain what you have done with all that He has given you? Have you used it for His glory and the benefit of His kingdom? Share with your group one area where you need to improve—time, money, possessions, giftedness, etc., and one way you can improve in that area.

- ***Diamonds in the Word:*** Somewhere in your study Bible or commentary may be a list of parables that Jesus told. Carefully look over the list. Read those that seem to relate to this parable and write down Jesus' points.

29.***Responding to God:*** James 1:5 promises that God will give us wisdom when we ask. Write a

prayer asking for wisdom in handling all the blessings that God has given you. Listen for His answer.

AMY'S STORY

I grew up in churches where my mom was always
the organist and I was given the opportunity to play
piano in the main service on a regular basis. I took it for
granted and assumed that wherever I went, I would be
given the same opportunity. I knew that I had the ability
and looked forward to using my skills at Northwest
Bible.

When I started attending, I met with and audi-
tioned for all the right people and was told that I would
get to play. Month after month went by and I started
getting frustrated because I wasn't given the opportunity
I expected. (It didn't help that the church pianist was far
more talented than me!) I finally "resolved" that I would
even play for the children's choir, which to me was set-

tling for less than I deserved. Even then, they still didn't use me! What a blow that was to my ego.

I finally had to say, "Lord, I don't know what you're doing, but you've given me these gifts and I want you to use them where you need me." Shortly thereafter, I was asked to play on a new worship team. Quite honestly, we were awful and I was somewhat embarrassed. But little did I realize the doors that would open because of my obedience to start playing with that worship team.

It was extremely humbling when I was asked to play in the main worship service on Sundays. My attitude was 180 degrees from where it had been when I started attending. I've actually lost some of my technical ability that I had through college so it has really caused me to lean heavily on God to provide the skills to play week after week.

My pride kept me from playing for some time, but God was able to use me once my heart was in the right place. My playing is His gift to use for His glory!

Coming Home to Jesus

Week Nine—Come Home to Your King

A PRECIOUS WORD FROM GOD

"Blessed is the King who comes in the name
of the Lord."

Spoken about Jesus in Luke 19:38 (NET)

INTRODUCTION

We have followed Jesus through His Galilean ministry and on the journey to Jerusalem. Finally, He
reached the end of the journey where He spent the final

days before His death teaching the people who gathered for the Passover Feast. Hear Him as He reached out, seeking them. Watch as many of His own people rejected Him as their King.

DAY ONE STUDY

Read Luke 19:28-40.

This event must be understood in the light of Jesus' heritage. Remember that He was the descendant of David, in the line of the Jewish kings. He was the rightful King of the Jews, promised throughout the Old Testament and anticipated as the one to bring them freedom from foreign oppression.

1. In the light of this background, why was it significant that the crowds called him their king? Memorize the **Precious Word from God**.

2. Contrast the response of the disciples in the crowd to that of the Pharisees.

The *NET Bible* comments on Jesus' words in Luke 19:40: "I tell you, if they keep silent, the very stones will cry out!"[20]

> This statement amounts to a rebuke. The idiom of creation speaking means that even creation knows what is taking place, yet the Pharisees miss it.

> NET Bible

3. ***Sharing question:*** Have you come home to Jesus as your king? Do you bow the knee and accept His will in your life? Do you see Him as your ruler? How can you measure your allegiance to Him as your King and to His kingdom?

---

[20] *NET Bible* Note 8, p. 1867.

- *Diamonds in the Word:* Read in your commentaries concerning this triumphal entry into Jerusalem. Write down your insights about the significance of this event.

Read Luke 19:41-44.

4. Why did Jesus weep over Jerusalem?

Have you recognized that God visited you in Jesus? Have you seen His work in your life? Have you responded to the fact that He came seeking you? If not, Jesus weeps over you, just as He did over this city. He calls out and asks you to believe in Him by trusting Him to forgive you of all your sins and bring you home to God.

5. *Sharing question:* Consider how you may miss God at work right in front of you, just as these Jewish leaders did. Perhaps you believe that He is at work, but you get so busy and involved in your own life that you fail to notice what He is doing

around you. Or perhaps you have your own agenda for His work and do not accept anything else as being from Him. Are you really aware of God's presence and His speaking to you daily? What can you do to become more in tune with the work and the voice of God?

6. ***Responding to God:*** Spend the rest of your time simply listening to what God wants to say to you about your sensitivity to His presence, His voice, and His work in the world.

Dr. Tim Sykes

DAY TWO STUDY

Read Luke 19:45-48.

7. Why did Jesus drive out those selling in the temple?

- **Diamonds in the Word:** Do some research into the buying and selling going on in the temple. Use commentaries, study Bibles, Bible encyclopedias, etc.

8. In light of Jesus' comments, what problems do you see with making it convenient to buy the animals and other items needed for sacrifices?

9. Can you think of any way that we may detract from worship in our churches today, as those buying and selling in the temple did then?

10.Luke 19:47-48 describes this final week in Jesus' life in a general way. Contrast what was going on with the people with what the leaders were doing.

Dr. Bock helps us understand the significance of the cleansing of the temple at this point in the story:[21]

------

[21] Bock, 317.

The connection between Jesus 'entry and his first public act in the temple should not be ignored. The linkage makes Jesus' act one of messianic and prophetic authority. . . A prophet who also saw himself as a king had to be stopped, especially if he was going to impose himself on the nation's worship.

Darrell Bock in *Luke*

11. ***Sharing question:*** As believers, our bodies are God's temple today, under His authority rather than our own (1 Cor. 6:19-20). In what ways do you fail to use your body for God's glory—failure to eat properly, failure to exercise, sex outside of marriage, looking at things you should not see, etc.? Commit to one change that you will make to-day to drive this out of your life.

12. ***Responding to God:*** Write a prayer committing this to God.

DAY THREE STUDY

Read Luke 20:1-8.

13. How did the Jewish leaders confront Jesus?

14. What did their answer and their reasoning reveal about them?

Read Luke 20:9-19.

This story is likely an allegory rather than a parable because of the great number of points that correspond with reality.[22]

- **Diamonds in the Word:** Go through the allegory writing down each point in the story and then relating them to reality. Explain why this is an allegory rather than a parable.

15. Explain Jesus' allegory. How was it directed against the leaders?

Read Luke 20:20-26.

16. How did Jesus avoid the trickery of the leaders?

---

[22] Bock, 321.

17. ***Sharing question:*** Jesus outsmarted the smartest of the nation's leaders over and over. His words reveal His great wisdom. In what area do you need Him to give you wisdom today? Why?

18. ***Responding to God:*** Write a prayer expressing your desire to avoid the kind of unbelief that these leaders showed throughout Jesus' ministry.

DAY FOUR STUDY

Read Luke 20:27-40.

The Sadducees did not believe in either the resurrection or in angels.[23]

- ***Diamonds in the Word:*** Use your resource materials to learn more about the Sadducees and their beliefs.

19. How did Jesus' reply suggest that they were wrong in all these beliefs?

Read Luke 20:41-44.

---

[23] Bock, 325.

Jesus turned the tables on the leaders who kept trying to trick Him with their questions by asking them a question. David's descendants were in the line of the kings and the expected Messiah; even these leaders believed that Messiah would come from the Davidic line.

20. Read Psalm 110 from which this quote comes. What did David tell us about the Messiah?

21. Read Acts 2:22-39 and Luke 22:69. How would you answer Jesus' question to the Sadducees?

Read Luke 20:45-21:4.

22. Contrast the attitudes that Jesus condemned in the leaders and the attitude He commended in the widow.

23. **Sharing question:** Something in us loves attention, popularity, and success; thus, these desires motivate our actions. Think of one action you have taken in order to achieve personal honor and share it with your group. If you are unsure, think of a time when no one noticed something you did and you were upset at being overlooked.

24.***Responding to God:*** Confess the sin of seeking personal honor to God. Ask Him for the grace to recognize this in yourself when it surfaces.

DAY FIVE STUDY

Today's lesson is full of Jesus' teaching about the future. Someday we may cover Jesus' prophecies in detail; however, today all we can do is look at some of His main points. In order to better understand them, you may find Dr. Bock's comments helpful:[24]

Jesus' eschatological discourse links together two such events, the destruction of Jerusalem in A.D. 70 and the events of the end sig-

---

[24] Bock, 333.

naling his return to earth. Because the events are patterned after one another and mirror one another, some of Jesus' language applies to both. . . . Luke clearly shows how the destruction of A.D. 70 is distinct from but related to the end. The two events should not be confused, but Jerusalem's destruction, when it comes, will guarantee as well as picture the end, since an event mirrors the other. Both are a part of God's plan as events move toward the end.

Darrell Bock in Luke

Read Luke 21:5-28.

25. List some of the main events predicted in the discourse. Consider each one and whether it seems to relate to the destruction of Jerusalem in A.D. 70 or the time of Jesus' return. Write down your understanding of each.

26. What questions do you have about these events? Sometimes I find it helpful to write down my confusion so that I can think about it later. There won't be time in your small group to answer these, but at least you will clearly know what you don't know.

- **Diamonds in the Word:** Compare this discourse with the ones in Matthew 24:1-35 and Mark 13:1-37.

.

Read Luke 21:29-38.

27. What attitudes are Christ-followers to have while waiting for the events that have not yet occurred?

28.***Sharing question:*** What we truly believe affects how we live. How do your actions show that you believe a day of judgment is coming or that you do not really believe it?

29.***Responding to God:*** Over and over in this lesson we have seen the authority of Jesus, the Messiah and King, revealed. Bow the knee before Him and give Him your allegiance, just as you have seen a knight do before a king. He deserves all of your loyalty. Write down your prayer.

As Jesus cleaned out the temple to restore true worship, there may be areas in our lives that need cleaning out so that God may rule there and we are truly home.

CARRI'S STORY

A while back, I asked the Lord to show me sin in my life that needed to be "cleaned out," so that I could grow closer to Him in my walk. He began to convict me of being judgmental and critical of a few people in my life. These people were ones that I had a very hard time dealing with and relating to. We were different in our beliefs and ways of living. I knew that they were in my life for a reason and some would be in my life forever. I really needed to get my heart right about them and I was becoming bitter toward them. It was painful and tiring to hold bitterness toward them and I knew I needed to let it go and give it to the Lord.

I grew up in a Christian home and had very strong "black and white" convictions about things. I felt like everyone should believe the way I did and should stay away from things that I considered sin for my life. I became critical of Christians who did things that I felt were wrong and began to judge them in their faith.

The Lord began to show me that I needed to give these people the kind of grace (undeserved favor) that He has given me through His son, Jesus. I knew I could not do it on my own, because I had tried and I always ended up frustrated with these people and I would fail at showing them grace. So I prayed that the Lord would work through me to clean out this sin in me.

I also turned to His Word for guidance and began to see how merciful and compassionate the Lord is to us even thought we are sinners and don't deserve it. The scriptures that He gave me that really helped me to see his grace and convict me of my judging others were: Exodus 34:6 "The Lord, The Lord, the compassionate and gracious God, slow to anger, abounding in love and faithfulness, maintaining love to thousands, and forgiving wickedness, rebellion and sin." Also Matthew 7:1-5 "Do not judge, or you too will be judged. For in the same way you judge others, you will be judged, and with the measure you use, it will be measured to you. Why do you speak of sawdust in your brother's eye and pay not attention to the plank in your own eye? How can you say to your brother, 'Let me take the speck out to your eye,' when all the time there is a plank in your own eye? You hypocrite, first take the plank out of your own eye, and then you will see clearly to remove the speck from your brother's eye." These verses really convicted my heart and revealed my sin to me even more.

He also showed me through an evangelism training class that we are called as believers to reach out to the lost and not judge them for the sin in their life. How could I ever bring someone to Christ if I could not get past their sin to show them the love of Jesus? Being critical of them would not be a good witness to them of what a Christian is like. They might say, "If that is what a Christian is like, than forget it!" In Matthew 9:12 Jesus says "It is not the healthy who need a doctor, but the sick. But go and learn what this means: 'I desire mercy, not sacrifice,' for I have not come to call the righteous, but sinners."

I have been justified by His grace and I wanted to give that grace to those people in my life! Over the past few weeks I have learned so much about God's grace for me and through prayer and reading His word, He is strengthening me to show that grace to these people in my life. I have had such a peace around them and desire to just love them. My feelings and attitude have really changed toward them. I don't have the bitterness toward them that I use to have. I know that the Lord wanted this sin out of my life and by my obedience to Him he has "cleaned me out "and filled me up with more of Him. I know that there will be challenging times again with these people, but I will lean on the Lord to give me His grace, so that I can pass that grace on to them.

Dr. Tim Sykes

Coming Home to Jesus

Week Ten—Come Home and Believe in Jesus

A PRECIOUS WORD FROM GOD

"Thus it stands written that the Messiah would suffer and would rise from the dead on the third day, and repentance for the forgiveness of sins would be proclaimed in his name to all nations, beginning from Jerusalem."

Jesus in Luke 24:46-47 (NET)

INTRODUCTION

This is our last week studying the story of Jesus from the gospel of Luke. I pray that God has used it in your life to draw you closer to Him. This week's lesson covers the crucial section of Luke from the Last Supper through the Resurrection. Several weeks ago we saw that Jesus expressed His mission as coming to seek and to save the lost. On the cross He accomplished the salvation of mankind.

Many of you, like me, probably saw the movie *The Passion*. As you go through these Scriptures, that experience will give you a visual image of what happened during the last hours of Jesus' life. Don't rush through this lesson, but meditate upon Jesus' death for you and for me. He died that we might live and come home to God forever.

DAY ONE STUDY

Read Luke 22:1-6.

1. Why did the chief priests and lawyers need Judas?

Read Luke 22:7-38.

Many of us who have been in church for a long time know this story so well that we read it quickly and miss its significance. Take the time to reread it as if you were there at this final Passover dinner.

- **Diamonds in the Word:** Research the Jewish Passover Seder, which was first celebrated in Exodus 12, as the last plague fell on the Egyptians before the Jews departed the land. If you can get information about the actual observance of this meal today, consider how it pictures Jesus. Write down your insights.

The cup and the bread are traditionally pictures of a covenant, the most binding agreement made between parties. A marriage is a covenant, and God's relationship with His people is based upon covenant. That means that His promises are permanent and binding. Covenant involves oneness in relationship. When we partake of the bread and the cup we acknowledge our unity with Jesus.

2. Read 1 Cor. 11:20-34. To participate in communion is a serious matter. What was the problem with how they were participating in the Corinthian church? What do you learn from this passage about the seriousness of communion?

3. *Sharing question:* How do you make sure that you have the right attitude when you accept the bread and the cup?

4. Give practical examples of how church leaders fulfill Jesus' teaching about leadership in Luke 22:24-27 and John 13:12-17.

5. In what ways did Jesus encourage His followers while at the same time warning them (Luke 22:28-38)?

Dr. G. Campbell Morgan comments on Jesus' words:[25]

"Jesus said, 'It is enough.' He was not referring to the two swords, but to the conversation. It was an abrupt dismissal. He dismissed the subject, and immediately left the city, and went to Olivet."

Dr. G. Campbell Morgan in *The Gospel According to Luke*

6. ***Responding to God***: Consider the words of encouragement that you just read. How does God use them to encourage you today? Write your prayer of response to Him.

---

[25] G. Campbell Morgan, *The Gospel According to Luke* (Westwood, NJ: Fleming H. Revell, Co., 1931), 249.

DAY TWO STUDY

Read Luke 22:39-46.

7. What do you learn on this occasion from Jesus' example concerning prayer?

- **Diamonds in the Word:** Read Heb. 5:7-9, likely a description of Jesus' time in the Garden of Gethsemane. Read your notes and commentaries and write down your insights on these verses as well as those of Luke 22:40-46.

Read Luke 22:47-62.

8. Jesus warned the disciples not to fall into temptation in 22:40. What temptations did they fall into just afterward?

9. What emotions do you suppose Jesus and the disciples felt when He was arrested? Carefully read the passage to support your answer. What did Peter's emotions lead him to do?

10.*Sharing question:* What emotions tend to lead you into temptation—fear, anger, frustration, impatience? What sins in your life sometimes follow those emotions?

11. ***Sharing question***: In what situations or with what people are you most likely to deny Jesus in some form or fashion? Why?

12. ***Responding to God:*** The example of Jesus' forgiveness of Peter's denial is such an encouragement because we all fall short of giving Christ the allegiance He deserves. Write a prayer asking God to give you the grace and strength that you need to give Him your full allegiance, particularly in those situations you mentioned in #10.

DAY THREE STUDY

Read Luke 22:63-71.

13. Of what did the Jewish council of elders accuse Jesus? Who did He claim to be?

- **Diamonds in the Word:** Jesus quoted Psalm 110 to the Jewish council at His trial. Study the entire Psalm. Why did this quote upset them so? You are free to read any notes that you have on this passage.

Read Luke 23:1-25.

14. Compare the accusations brought against Jesus before Pilate with those the Jewish council considered. Why might they be different?

15. Describe Pilate and Herod's reactions to Jesus.

16. Describe the treatment of Jesus throughout the trials from Luke 22:63-23:24.

17. Read 1 Peter 2:19-25. Jesus is our example of enduring suffering. How does Peter teach us to follow Christ's example when we suffer mistreatment?

18. *Sharing question:* With what person in your life are you most likely to respond poorly when she/ he treats you badly? Perhaps your boss belittles you or embarrasses you. Maybe it is a parent or a sibling whose words or actions really get to you. What specific part of Jesus' example can you incorporate into your response next time, relying upon the Holy Spirit to help?

19.**Responding to God:** Spend time thanking Jesus for enduring suffering and ridicule for you. Thank Him for the great salvation that He bought for you. Write out a prayer or a poem of thanksgiving and praise.

DAY FOUR STUDY

Read Luke 23:26-31.

20. Even on His way to the cross, Jesus showed love and concern for the women of Jerusalem. Review Luke 21:20-24. What events did He foresee that caused Him sadness over these women?

Read Luke 23:32-56.

21. Consider these people that Luke describes who followed Jesus to the cross or attended the crucifixion. Write down their attitudes and reactions toward Jesus and His execution:

Rulers—

Soldiers—

HOLY WOMEN

1st criminal—

2nd criminal—

Centurion—

Crowds—

Those who knew Jesus—

Joseph of Arimathea—

The women who followed Him from Galilee—

Jesus died for every one of these people, whether they loved Him or rejected Him.

22. Why did Jesus willingly accept death? Read these verses and write down your insights:

    a. Rom. 5:6-10

    b. 1 Peter 1:18-19

    c. Hebrews 10:10-18

    d. Hebrews 12:1-2

23. *Sharing question:* What friends, co-workers, or family members of yours have rejected Jesus?

Name one practical way that you can show each
one His love, the kind of love that dies for those
who reject that love, the kind of love that draws us
home to Jesus.

- **Diamonds in the Word:** Study your resources and
  read about the temple and the curtain that was torn
  in two (Luke 23:45). Read Hebrews 8-10 in reference
  to this. What significance do you see in this act?

24.**Responding to God:** Draw a picture of a cross
   and put yourself before it. (Stick figures are great!)
   Depict your attitude toward Jesus in where you
   place yourself and what you are doing in the picture. Some of you are still on the journey to faith
   and have not yet believed in Him. Others of you
   are near but not bowed down. Are you home with
   Him?

DAY FIVE STUDY

Read Luke 24:1-12.

What an amazing gift these women received for their devotion to Jesus—to be the first to learn of His resurrection and the first to speak forth the good news!

25. How did the disciples react to the announcement by the women? How was Peter's reaction different?

Read Luke 24:13-35.

26. Describe the encounter between Jesus and the two men.

27. By the time these two reached Jerusalem, there had been another appearance of Jesus. For what reason might Jesus have sought out Peter and appeared to him alone?

Read Luke 24:36-53.

28. What message was given to Jesus' followers to share with the nations?

Have you believed in the message of Jesus? Do you believe that He is who He claimed to be—God? Do you need Him to cleanse you of all your sins and bring you home to the Father today and eventually forever? Will you trust in Him alone as your Way home?

- *Diamonds in the Word:* Outline the gospel message as you would share it with a friend who wanted to hear about your faith. What verses and illustrations would you use? Use tracts or other outlines with which you are familiar. If you have time, compare some of their differences for strengths and weaknesses.

29.*Sharing question:* Read Romans 10:14-17. We are allowed the great privilege of being His messengers. For those of you who have believed in Jesus already, how are you doing in sharing His message? Who in your life needs you to share the truth with her or him?

30.**Sharing question:** Share one way that God has changed you as you have studied the story of Jesus in Luke.

31.**Responding to God:** Write a prayer thanking God for your great salvation and the dear cost that Jesus paid to give this gift to you.

Dr. Tim Sykes

Just as the women who went to the tomb early that Sunday morning had the privilege of announcing the truth of Jesus' resurrection, we have the same honor as we share the gospel. Although God does not need us, He chooses to work through ordinary people like you and me. Michelle recounts the way that she reminds herself of this great privilege.

MICHELLE'S STORY

I have a picture on my refrigerator that reminds me of what a privilege it is to share the gospel of Jesus with others. It is a picture of a beautiful sixteen year old Haitian girl. The countenance of her face exhibits the power of the good news. This girl was the only one of small group that we were sharing with in Haiti who prayed to accept Jesus as her Savior. This group had been particularly negative that day. She was the youngest of the group. When the Holy Spirit spoke to her, she was bold enough to step forward and say she believed. On that Sunday she attended to first church service held in Roberts Village. Her sweet face reminds me of the privilege of being a part of the harvest.

BIBLIOGRAPHY

Bock, Darrell L. *Luke*, ed. Grand R. Osborne, The IVP New Testament Commentary Series, vol. 3. Downers Grove, IL: InterVarsity Press, 1994.

Morgan, G. Campbell. *The Gospel According to Luke.* Westwood, NJ: Fleming H. Revell, Co., 1931.

NET Bible: New English Translation, Second Beta Edition. Biblical Studies Press

About the Author

PASTOR TIMMY L. SYKES

Rev. Dr. Timmy L. Sykes is 49 years old and was born June 1, 1966 on the Island of Galveston, Texas. Rev Timmy Sykes is a former senior law enforcement officer with Galveston Police Department, and the Chattanooga Housing Authority Police Department, where he served as the Senior Criminal Investigator over the Fraud Investigations Unit [total of 25 years law enforcement, including having served and received an Honorable Discharge from the U. S. Army, Infantry School, Fort Benning, GA). Tim is married to Dr. Kathy Calloway-Sykes, D. Ph, MBA, They have a son named Thomas Josiah, and a Son; Tyler Lundale Sykes, who resides in Friendswood, TX.

After much prayer, Rev. Sykes relocated to Chattanooga, TN in July of 2002 and began serving as the Interim Pastor of Mount Canaan Missionary Baptist Church, after the retirement of Pastor Melvin Jordan.

On October 8, 2005 Pilgrim Rock Missionary Baptist Church called Rev. Timmy Sykes to serve as their Senior Pastor, and he is currently serving. Rev. Sykes previously served as Congress President of the Greater Pilgrim Joy District Association of Churches, and in August, 2010 was elected as Moderator of the Greater Pilgrim Joy District Association of Churches (12 churches).

May, 1984- Graduate: High School Diploma, Texas City High School, Texas City, TX.

May, 1991- Certificate of Course Completion; Biblical Studies: Conroe Normal & Industrial College of Biblical Studies, (extended branch campus; Texas City, TX)

May, 2000- Honorary Doctorate Degree (Honoris Causa)-Doctor of - Divinity, Conroe Normal & Industrial College of Biblical Studies, (extended branch campus; Texas City, TX)

December, 2002-Graduate: Bachelor of Science Degree in Business Administration, Trinity University- San Antonio, TX.

Made in the USA
Middletown, DE
22 March 2024